Teaching

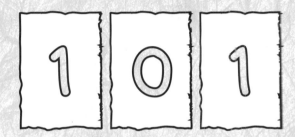

1 0 1

Devotions for Christian Teachers

Edward Grube

CPH
SAINT LOUIS

To Alana—God's little design

Copyright © 1999 Concordia Publishing House
3558 S. Jefferson Avenue, St. Louis, MO 63118-3968
Manufactured in the United States of America

1 2 3 4 5 6 7 8 9 10   08 07 06 05 04 03 02 01 00 99

Contents

Introduction

Dear Teacher,

I hope you find this assignment acceptable. I had lots of help from my Father, and my Brother did all the background work. The Holy Spirit sent many thoughts my way too. With those confessions out of the way, please accept *Teaching 101* as written especially for you.

I know your life is busy, dear teacher, so I'll keep each devotion brief. The best part will be God's Word. Perhaps my words will help you meditate on what God has done for you. I hope they will nourish your faith and bring a smile to your face too.

Each meditation in this book connects God's Word with some facet of your life as a teacher. I hope the messages will couple the routines of your ministry with God's love and care for you. After all, He made you what you are. You have a divine design!

God bless you, dear teacher!

Edward Grube

Teaching 101

Teaching 101

How long has it been since you labored through a foundations course? The more time you've spent in classrooms, the more you probably realize how much a foundation foundations are. Teachers succeed over time because they build on basic educational foundations. Christian teachers succeed because they rely on *the* foundation for every other foundation—Jesus Christ.

Someone once defined the teacher's task as taking a roomful of live wires and thoroughly grounding them. No, not as in "no recess for six months," but as in grounding them in the fundamentals of what they need to live their lives to the fullest.

> By the grace God has given me, I laid a foundation as an expert builder, and someone else is building on it. But each one should be careful how he builds. For no one can lay any foundation other than the one already laid, which is Jesus Christ.
>
> *1 Corinthians 3:10–11*

Teachers once did that for you. Perhaps your parents did too. The people that did it best were those who, by the power of the Holy Spirit, taught you about Jesus. They filled your foundation with faith-nurturing essentials—how Jesus suffered and died for your sins, how He rose again to defeat death, how He has returned to heaven to prepare a mansion for you, how He will come again to take you home. Now you have a God-given opportunity and privilege, even a responsibility, to tell others this Good News. This is part of a divine design tailored for you.

God made you what you are, and He called you to do what you are doing. He sent His Spirit to give you faith—faith onto which you build everything else As a Christian educator, the Spirit uses you to share the Gospel with your students and their families. Your task is to take those live wires in your classroom and ground them in Jesus' love.

God's divine design gives you some distinct advantages that help you serve Him and benefit others. With soul firmly planted in faith, you can influence lives beyond the usual influences that other teachers exert. You are an instrument of the Holy Spirit. God has given you relationships with students that need not end when they leave your classroom. Or your school. Or your world. The kids you see every day are the same faces that you may see throughout eternity. Only then, you'll be without the missed assignments, bickering, and recess rowdiness, which sometimes color your opinion of the ministry God gave you. Sort of like the lion resting with the lamb.

Prayer

Dear God, thank You for my divine design. Dear Jesus, thank You for being part of the Father's divine design for me. Dear Holy Spirit, help me use my divine design to glorify God and to serve others. Amen.

You Could Have Been ...

Today's Bible passage names some roles that God gives to His people. Perhaps as you read the verse, you mused that your current ministry makes you like the proverbial multiple-choice answer: all of the above. Though that doesn't really fit the meaning of the passage, the roles you play do have parallels to the passage.

> In the church God has appointed first of all apostles, second prophets, third teachers, then workers of miracles, also those having gifts of healing, those able to help others, those with gifts of administration, and those speaking in different kinds of tongues.
>
> *1 Corinthians 12:28*

Apostles had unique divine designs. God chose them for a highly specialized ministry of preaching, teaching, and dynamic leadership. By the power of the Holy Spirit, these men made disciples of many people, who in turn made disciples of more people, who in turn somewhere down a long time line nurtured your faith as the Word was shared. Now it's your turn to nurture the faith of those around you. You don't qualify as one of the original apostles, but you are an apostle of the story of salvation.

Are you a prophet? Sometimes as you watch your students, you can tell what is about to happen—the student about to fail, the child about to fall off the swing, the hurt feelings about to erupt in a torrent of tears. But that's experience, not prophecy. You do know one thing about the future though. You know what will happen when the final bell signals eternal dismissal. You know that Jesus will come again, this time to take you to heaven. You know you'll see lots of your kids there too.

Are you a worker of miracles? Well, you did help Richie pass last year! And you were the only one to notice that Wilma needed glasses. Then there were all those tears that you made disappear with a single, loving word. The greatest miracle, however, is one that you have experienced personally—forgiveness of sins. Because you are forgiven by God, you can forgive others.

The last roles the passage mentions may be those that completely elude you. However, you manage a classroom, grade book, lesson plans, book money, and probably things far more frustrating. You are an administrator! But speaking in tongues? Maybe that's best left to a bilingual teacher. But you do speak a language unique to Christian teachers. You speak the love of Christ. That's one language everyone needs to hear.

Prayer

Thank You, Father, for rolling so many roles into my life. Thank You for designing me with distinctive skills for serving the children in my classroom. Thank You for making me a teacher. Amen.

3

You Could Have Been a Plumber

Don't feel badly if the closest you've been to plumbing is the faucet display in Sears. (If you sit down and think about it, you've actually been much closer!) If you've never tried plumbing, count yourself smarter than others who have ventured the statement, "It's only a little leak. I'll fix it myself." Real plumbers are worth their weight in washers!

Since my youth, O God, You have taught me, and to this day I declare Your marvelous deeds.

Psalm 71:17

Teachers are plumbers even if the only wrench they've handled is the one that afflicted their backs after moving a box of textbooks. After all, you know much about the cure for leaky eyes, the foibles of drinking fountains, the dynamics of Thermos bottle threads, and the utter necessity of potty breaks in suitable proportion to grade level. But your most important plumbing task involves extending God's pipeline of blessings from Scripture into the lives of others.

God's pipeline to us was more difficult to build than the one that runs through Alaska. His pipeline crossed mountains of sin and frigid wastelands of enmity. It survived violent quaking from Satan and the severe storms of human temptations. Miraculously, only one death resulted from the project. Tragically, it was God's Son who died. But that was no accident; it was part of God's divine design to save sinners.

What flows through God's pipeline? He showers us with forgiveness and engulfs us with blessings. Therefore, say with the psalmist, "I declare Your marvelous deeds." And we can announce these words of praise to the tender ears of kids who sit in our classrooms. Even if circumstances prohibit actual words of praise, we can spray ample doses of Godly love and forgiveness on our students. And we can point to the pipeline the Holy Spirit has built between child and God.

Pipelines run two ways. We not only have a pipeline *from* God but one *to* Him. Through it, we channel our prayers. God listens to us, but He knows our needs and the needs of others better than we do. He answers our prayers in better ways than we can imagine. In fact, He knows what's coming down the pipe even before we send our prayer to Him. Take time now to pump your concerns to Him. Be sure to tell Him about your students too.

Prayer

Dearest Jesus, thank You for taking away my sins and connecting me directly to God. Let Your blessings flow freely to me and to my students. Amen.

You Could Have Been an Airline Pilot

A sage traveler once said, "You can't fool all the people all the time, but airline schedules make a valiant attempt." Air travel enables middle-school teachers to whisk their students to the nation's capital four or more years ahead of when many of us made our first visit.

> You guide me with Your counsel, and afterward You will take me into glory. *Psalm 73:24*

Air travel has made it possible to shrink the world so we can eat lunch in Chicago and get indigestion in San Francisco! So why would you want to be an airline pilot?

Maybe you never thought of this change in profession, but it could be lucrative. First, consider this: Although pilots make lots of money, their lives are frequently up in the air. (Go ahead and groan. It will do you about as much good as griping about flight delays.) As far as qualifications, pilots must be smart, responsible, and conscientious. After all, they are taking people places, speeding through a hostile environment, and encountering and overcoming difficult obstacles.

Doesn't that sound a little like your job? Teachers must be smart, responsible, and conscientious. After all, they are taking children places, speeding (okay, sometimes creeping) through a hostile environment, and encountering and overcoming difficult obstacles. But where are you taking the children?

By God's grace, you take children where you already have been, a place you visit daily. You take them to the foot of the cross. You've been there many more times than they have, so you're familiar with the terrain. You know just where to lay your sins. You hear the words of forgiveness, and you prance away as happy as a fourth-grader leaving a museum gift shop. But do you remember your first visit?

God brought you to the cross that first time through Baptism. He sent the Holy Spirit to counsel you, and now you soar with the joy of salvation. I hope your students already have boarded the flight to glory at the baptismal font. Some probably have not. Others never will.

So do what many passengers do when they board an airplane. Snap the seat belt and say lots of prayers. Then show your students the cockpit and tell them all you know about getting from point A to glory.

Prayer

O Holy Spirit, use me. Use me to teach my students about eternal life with You. Make us soar swiftly on the wings of Jesus' death and triumphant resurrection. Bring us safely home. Amen.

You Could Have Been a Physician

What prevented you from becoming a doctor? Was it the long years of med school or the frightening prospect of malpractice insurance? Maybe it was blood and other disgusting messes that physicians routinely confront. So you became a teacher instead. The only real difference is the long years of medical school. And, of course, the pay.

> But in your hearts set apart Christ as Lord. Always be prepared to give an answer to everyone who asks you to give the reason for the hope that you have. But do this with gentleness and respect. *1 Peter 3:15*

You are a healer who is assisting the Great Physician. You heal hurt feelings, learning deficiencies, and poor self-images. You've suffered from all these maladies before. All these ailments characterize a sin-sick world, and you have suffered them personally. You've felt the sting of sin and recognized your inability to impress God with your goodness. Your soul was sick and dying. But the Great Physician came to your aid and gave you hope. He didn't berate you with your sinfulness; He gently forgave you instead. And because of what He did, God finds you respectable and righteous.

The Great Physician affords a model for Christian teachers. It would not be proper for you to practice medicine on children, but it is proper to practice healing. All your students suffer from sin, and you possess the only miracle remedy. The prescription is priceless, but it's also free. Forgiveness heals and offers hope. All too often it's an uncommon cure. The world of unbelievers refuses to practice it and fails to understand it. Perhaps that's not so bad because maybe they'll ask about it.

Christians are different. People notice these differences. Occasionally, these differences will result in insult, mockery, the "I can't believe it" head shake, or an unreasonable expectation of perfect behavior. That's something you live with, just as you live with upset parents calling during supper or writing inflammatory notes. While there doesn't seem to be much hope in situations like that, your daily example of Christ's love and forgiveness gets noticed, even in difficult situations. One day, when someone really needs you (even grudgingly), God will open their hearts and you'll get to tell them of your hope. When that happens, think like a doctor. Be gentle.

Prayer

Lord Jesus, thank You for healing me of my sinfulness. I suffer from it daily, but You never tire of treating me with forgiveness. Who needs the caduceus? We have the cross! Amen.

6

You Could Have Been an Accountant

The main principle of accounting is that for every debit there must be a credit. Everyone and anyone could be an accountant if it ended there. But accountants complicate things by including topics such as subaccounts, amortization, depreciation, accounts payable, accounts receivable, collection agencies, and large men in dark bulging suits carrying cement bags, and ... Well, that's only if your credits don't match your debits, so let's not get carried away—at least by the guys in dark suits!

Blessed is the man whose sin the Lord *does not count against him and in whose spirit is no deceit. Psalm 32:2*

Perhaps you should have taken an accounting course in preparation for teaching. You do a lot of number crunching, particularly at report card time. And at 11 P.M., when you're calculating averages and you can no longer focus on the tiny numbers in your grade book, you know for sure why you didn't become an accountant.

Grades aren't the only way you practice

the educational form of accounting. Maybe you're responsible for everything from collecting overdue book fines to keeping track of milk money and odd-amount fees ($4.37?!) for the next field trip.

One thing you don't have to count are sins—yours or your students. Can you imagine the size of the grade book just for you-know-who-in-the-first-row alone? Of course, your own sins wouldn't exactly be a pittance either. But listen to David's proclamation of God's life-saving credit: Our sins don't count against us!

In most schools, teachers give account of students' behavior through a grade, points, or a checklist. For students, the consequence of poor work habits or little preparation is a poor grade. (This may not go over well at home.) Of course, sin has consequences for your life too. Although you have suffered as a result of your sins, the real suffering took place on the cross. Multiply your suffering by what you really deserve, then multiply that product by the world's population (past, present and future) and ... You don't have to be an accountant to get the idea of how much sin cost Jesus!

Your sins are forgiven. Each experience of repentance and forgiveness brings you back to a zero balance. Be sure to adjust your students' ledgers every day just as God adjusts yours! It makes the accounting much simpler.

Prayer

Lord Jesus, thank You for taking away my sins. Help me forgive as I have been forgiven, especially in those tough situations when it's hard to forgive. In Your name I pray. Amen.

7

You Could Have Been a Rocket Scientist

You have heard the phrase "You don't have to be a rocket scientist to ..." Usually the little dots are replaced by a phrase naming an activity requiring few brain cells. For example, "You don't have to be a rocket scientist to remember to actually use the washroom on washroom break!"

Salvation is found in no one else, for there is no other name under heaven given to men by which we must be saved.

Acts 4:12

That familiar phrase tends to elevate the intelligence of rocket scientists. The implication is that rocket scientists have to be smarter than the average smart person. They must figure out how to fling an object into a designated area of outer space. For us more average types, perhaps we can equate that with finding a parking space at the mall during the final shopping days before Christmas.

Teachers are smart. Just ask any first-grader. (*Warning:* Do not ask an eighth-grader!) We have things figured out, and when we don't, we check the teacher's manual. Christian teachers have things figured out too, but we can't take credit for it. Even the teacher's manual would be beyond our grasp were it not for the Holy Spirit.

The primary gift of the Holy Spirit is the gift of faith. That's the element that puts us beyond human intelligence. Faith is the great equalizer that gives the same grace to the learning disabled as is given to those who shoot at the stars. Faith provides everything we need to live forever.

Those outside the faith think the list of things to know—and certainly the list of things to do—must be miles long! But we know better. We have a simple answer to the complex question: "What must I do to be saved?" Our answer? "Salvation is found in no one else!" Jesus is the name to know, and it's the only name that saves us. Sounds simple, doesn't it?

Sin muddles the simplicity though. Sin prompts us to pursue our doubts about God's love and His power over sin and the devil. So much doesn't make sense! How could God create people from dust or bring the Savior to life in the body of a virgin? It defies intelligence! Thank God for carrying us through such doubts. Thank God for leading us to repentance and opening our hearts to accept forgiveness. Thank God for making us smarter than we look!

Prayer

Thank You, Lord, for sending the Holy Spirit to give me faith in the only one I need to know for eternal life—Jesus. Empower me to share His name with others. Amen.

8

You Could Have Been a CEO

Maybe you never wanted to be one, but that's how it turned out. You are the chief executive officer of your classroom. (No matter what little Melinda says!) You spend your days managing, multitasking, moderating, musing, manufacturing, maneuvering, muttering ... Mmmm. Maybe that last one doesn't belong, but CEOs probably do it too.

If any of you lacks wisdom, he should ask God, who gives generously to all without finding fault, and it will be given to him. James 1:5

You make many decisions every day from your "executive office." Each decision impacts the lives of all those faces that look to you for guidance and knowledge. What you decide from moment to moment affects even those with the blank stares and the dream-glazed eyes—the kid studying aviation design with her ruler and pencil and the one researching the spread of disease by waving his tissue in the air. You decide on the spur of the moment how to answer Joanie's question about how her dog can have puppies or Joey's query about the theology of suicide. You make long-range decisions too. "It's raining this morning.

What will I do for recess?" Then there are the longest-range plans. "What if it rains again next week?"

What you do is far more significant than all that. Isn't it sometimes scary to grasp the real importance of the decisions you make? You're not always right, and that heaps guilt on your psyche. It also darkens your soul. Sin has that awful effect. In fact, making a few wrong decisions can paralyze your willingness to face decision-making situations. It's enough to make you thankful that you're not the CEO of General Motors or IBM! But you're not really off the hook. You are responsible for something far more important.

Sin paralyzes, but God's unearned love heals. His love through the work of Jesus enables you to persevere. His power through the Holy Spirit saturates you with wisdom to continue working for the good of those children watching you with expectant eyes (even if they are closed!). So boldly decide both the momentous and the mundane. Do what James recommends. Do it now.

Prayer

Dear God, I pray for wisdom. I know I don't deserve any special insight, but I ask You in the name of Jesus. I ask You despite my sins because Jesus has made me faultless in Your sight. Give me wisdom to make decisions that please You. Amen.

9

You Could Have Been a Street Person

If a school board member suggested today's title, you probably would be offended. Or at least frightened. Then again, considering your present salary, maybe the statement is closer to the truth than many could imagine.

For we do not have a high priest who is unable to sympathize with our weaknesses, but we have one who has been tempted in every way, just as we are—yet was without sin. *Hebrews 4:15*

Street people may possess a treasure that the more affluent may lack: They have "street smarts." They are wise to the world and shun it—sometimes by choice, sometimes by circumstance. Within their brand of wisdom often exists admirable characteristics such as compassion, which is most often demonstrated toward those in similar circumstances. Street people care for one another despite their own tremendous need. Have you ever wondered at the kindness and mercy that some street people extend to a stray dog or an abandoned cat?

You are like a street person. You, too, are wise to the world. As you grow in teaching experience, your students give you "street smarts." You know the ways of their world, and you care for one another. You understand your students' hurts and fears and weaknesses, and sometimes they understand yours. (Especially your weaknesses!) You have chosen to live this way, but there is more to it. You were chosen by God to minister to children. You were sent to them, even though you could have done something more awesome in the eyes of modern society.

Jesus came to us like a street person. He had no fixed home. He roamed the countryside with a band of friends. He didn't consider His own comfort. Instead, Jesus spent His time healing, supplying, comforting, and forgiving. Jesus was thrust into those circumstances by God, who knew our needs. And Jesus willingly went to the cross, not because He was too unmotivated or uneducated to do anything else. He went in obedience to His Father. He went because He loved us.

There are some aspects of street life that teachers would do well to emulate. Not because we're too lazy or too unskilled to do anything else. Rather because God sent us to minister to others with the same "street smarts" that Jesus applied to His life and, more important, to the lives of others.

Prayer

Lord Jesus, make me like You. As I weave through the desks in my classroom, help me think like my students and feel their needs. Give me the compassion and the smarts to know how best to help them. In Your name I pray. Amen.

10

You Could Have Been a Janitor

You know how important janitors are, and you really know how important they are when someone makes a mess!

Wash away all my iniquity and cleanse me from my sin. ... Cleanse me with hyssop, and I will be clean; wash me, and I will be whiter than snow.

Psalm 51:2, 7

Jesus had a terrible mess to clean up. It would have been bad if He had to cleanse only one sinner, but multiply that by all the people who have ever lived and who have yet to live. Then multiply that number by the number of sins. The product would make the national debt pale in comparison. Thinking about all those sinners and their sinfulness is a sterile exercise. If we focus on just one sinner, whom we know quite well, it's enough to make a messy point.

Jesus not only took away our sins, He made us clean—whiter than snow, the Bible says. Now we live as God's children, imperfect to be sure, but always clean by the blood Jesus sacrificed on Calvary. Doesn't being clean feel good? It's like that warm shower after a day in a stuffy classroom filled with sneezing kids who ate a lunch of peanut butter and jelly sandwiches and finger painted during art class.

We can enjoy our cleanliness, but we are called to do more with it than relax and feel good. We can share it the way we say we will in the Lord's Prayer. Jesus took away the sins of the world, which includes those who cough and write and read and sin before you every day. Although we can't deliver spiritual purity as Jesus did on the cross, we are His agents, capable of forgiving in His name. And that brings us to those whom we serve.

"Those whom we serve." Maybe we forget that concept occasionally. We are servants, and those whom we serve are 3 or 10 or 13. Like the janitor who serves us, our job is to keep things clean. A nearly impossible task! Why, it would take a miracle. And it did. Forgiveness for Jesus' sake is a miracle. Wiping away every smudge on our soiled souls was a miracle Plan to share that mysterious, powerful work of God today. Clean up one of those third-graders and polish that sixth-grader. Do it with the same tools Jesus used— grace, mercy, and love.

Prayer

Thank You, Lord, for making me clean. Help me to forgive as You have forgiven me. Amen.

11

The Best Days of Your Life

Close your eyes and think for a moment. (Go ahead. Someone will surely wake you—maybe the principal!) Think about the best days of your life. When were they? What happened that made them so good? Who else was involved? Did the day revolve around you or around someone else?

"For in Him we live and move and have our being." As some of your own poets have said, "We are His offspring." Acts 17:28

The remainder of the page could be blank because you probably have enough to meditate on, but let's put your best days in perspective. Many Christians feel obligated to name the day of their Baptism as the very best day. Perhaps *obligated* is too strong a word, but when you think of what you owe the Lord for His gift of salvation, the word makes sense. Baptism is that day on which we received faith to recognize and confess Jesus as our Savior. There was no other way for that to happen. So Baptism was, indeed, the best day (so far).

Among your best days, you might list your first day of class in your first classroom. (Then again, maybe there were better days!) There was that excitement, that feeling of responsibility, that rush of love for those unique young strangers left in your care. And care you did!

"Best" days also might be "last" days of school, celebration days, or middle-of-the-week days. Even a day like today might be a "best" day.

Ask your students the questions in the first paragraph. Did you share any common answers? Despite the variety of responses, all Christians have one thing in common. They share their feelings about God in much the same way in classrooms, homes, parks, ... Although Christian teachers have a unique mission to teach God's children, sometimes our personal witness becomes an oversight. And teachers in public education fear the consequences of talking about their Savior in public. Sin has creepy, subtle ways of keeping Christians in check. So ask God, who gave you the best day in your life, to continue giving you good days. The very best is yet to come.

Prayer

Dear Lord, thank You for sending the Holy Spirit into my life through Baptism. Wash me every day with the cleansing waters of forgiveness, and give me a role in helping my students have the best days of their lives too. Amen.

12

Who Is You?

Grammar teachers already have their red pens in hand! "Who *are* you?" they may insist. This meditation isn't asking you to define yourself. Rather, open your grade book and look at all the names. Which student is you? Which child reminds you of you?

Examine yourselves to see whether you are in the faith; test yourselves. Do you not realize that Christ Jesus is in you—unless, of course, you fail the test?

2 Corinthians 13:5

The apostle Paul told people to examine themselves. The test probably had mixed results. How would you come out? When you examine yourself, are you like that student who does bad things all day? Christians sometimes have that focus. They sag under the weight of guilt and indulge in a constant accounting of their wickedness. They feel helpless to change so they maintain that behavior. If they ask God for forgiveness, they often neglect to accept it and forgive themselves.

Maybe you're more like that student classified as "mischievous." That's the student who regularly misbehaves but is lovable anyway. She's the student about whom teachers say, "Oh, she tries sooooo hard to be good. She does the best she can." If your examination reveals this classification, remember that "trying hard" has nothing to do with success in God's course of life. He will not think it's cute that you try hard yet regularly succumb to mischief. Instead, He will forgive you, and He does it out of His totally unconditional love for Jesus' sake.

Perhaps you compare favorably with that good student in your class—the one who always greets you and completes his homework. Now there is you! Now there is danger! Good people, like you, face as many spiritual dangers as those "less good." Yet every sin nailed Jesus to the cross. When you're good, you also may be in grave danger. When you're so good, what is easy to forget?

Sin corrupts the lives of all. You don't need to compare yourself to the students in your class. You are uniquely you—good, bad, and otherwise. Jesus knows you. In fact, He recognizes Himself in you. As Paul says, "Christ Jesus is in you." What Jesus recognizes is the good part. He sees the you He bought on the cross. Whom does He recognize as one of His own? You.

Prayer

Thank You, Holy Spirit, for leading me to recognize and confess my sinfulness. Strengthen me that others may see Jesus' love and forgiveness at work in me. Amen.

On Display

I hope it's clear to you. God desires that everyone believe, and He has given all believers various roles to live on earth. He has called some to be truck drivers, others to be medical workers, and still others to be teachers. He has a divine design for everyone. He has designed you to teach, and He has provided an excellent model of how to do it.

> Do not repay anyone evil for evil. Be careful to do what is right in the eyes of everybody. If it is possible, as far as it depends on you, live at peace with everyone.
>
> *Romans 12:17–18*

You learned different teaching strategies in college and through experience. Educators enjoy talking about what they do to motivate children to learn, to pique excitement to succeed, even when working with those who appear to be the slowest learners. By now you probably know that how you act in class can be as important as what you teach. Your "self" is a teaching strategy too.

Under God's perfect plan, He designed all humans to be good teachers, only He had a different name for teachers. He called them parents. For centuries, Godly parents fulfilled that role. (Ungodly ones did too, but they didn't teach their children the same things.) These parents tutored their children and demonstrated useful skills. It's unlikely the parents were successful unless they also modeled what they taught. In that respect, education hasn't changed much.

Somewhere on the time line of pedagogy, the title of teacher was granted to adults other than parents. One thing didn't change, however; these adults needed to live what they taught. Good teachers always have done that. They get excited about ideas and skills because those things are important in their lives. Thank God for teachers like that!

Into what kind of teacher has God molded you? He has placed some of you in Christian classrooms where you have the additional privilege of teaching about God the Father, Jesus the Savior, and the Holy Spirit even as you educate your students about science, reading, and current events. Wherever God has placed you, wherever He has designed you to work, remember that teaching is more than telling. Remember Paul's words to the Romans.

Prayer

Make us model teachers, Lord. Give us the power to display Your love to all those we meet. Amen.

Graduate School

Have you heard about the two unemployed school teachers? One had no principle, and the other had no class. (Now you know why your students groan!)

> To prepare God's people for works of service, so that the body of Christ may be built up until we all reach unity in the faith and in the knowledge of the Son of God and become mature, attaining to the whole measure of the fullness of Christ. *Ephesians 4:12–13*

How do you feel about your former classes—the ones who have graduated from your level to the next? Were they as ready for the next grade as your new class was ready for yours? (Be careful how you answer!) Perhaps it's safer to think of graduates as works in progress. When you think about it, perhaps that's true of yourself as well.

You are in a perpetual graduate school. The goal of your education is in the words Paul wrote to the Ephesians. God invested His Son's life in your future to prepare you for works of service by the power of the Holy Spirit. You realize how wonderful that investment is only when you realize what a bad "student" you once were. Despite your sinfulness, God loved you and made you fit for service in His kingdom—service you now fulfill with friends, relatives, and students.

Isn't it good to know that you're not alone in this never-ending education? Paul uses the phrase "we all" to reveal the extent of God's kingdom. You have the company of many Christians with many callings as you reach together for unity of faith and spiritual maturity.

Christian teachers have a unique calling in the crowd of believers. Yours is a ministry to children, and your goal matches the one God has for you: to shape young souls and hearts into servants who mature throughout life as they learn and live God's Word.

How long will we be about this business? Until we reach fullness in Jesus! That may be a long way off. It may be only moments away. Whenever it happens, you will be ready to join with multitudes of believers for the greatest service ever—the moment when we praise our Savior at the gates of heaven. How's that for a graduation celebration!

Prayer

Dear Savior, thank You for giving me a heart to serve my students. Help me to mature and always give me the privilege of serving You as I serve others. Amen.

15

Sit Down

She must have been a master of quotations because you find many attributed to her. She had one about prayer that goes like this: "If Christians spent as much time praying as they do grumbling, they would soon have nothing to grumble about." That truth is from Anonymous.

I urge, then, first of all, that requests, prayers, intercession and thanksgiving be made for everyone. *1 Timothy 2:1*

Have you found yourself grumbling more often than you care to admit? Or more often than you realize? It's a common malady of all professions, including teaching. Of course, we can justify most of it.

The first grumble softly rumbles as we slide from our bed and remember that today we have a staff meeting after school for that squinty-eyed student who can't read. Why do we need an interdisciplinary team of specialists to break gently but firmly the news we already know: Sheila needs glasses!

The next grumble stirs our defenses. Why did Mr. Holland leave this note on my desk? Oh, it's only his Opus number 12 demanding better discipline from my students when he conducts music class! Then there is the other note, the one from Shelly's mother, which states that Shelly isn't "getting" math because I didn't teach it well. Someday Mrs. Crabb will realize just how lazy her daughter is!

Imagine God's right to grumble. He made a paradise where two perfect humans could live, and what do they do? And there were those children of Israel. God gave them food and drink in the desert, led them around with clouds and fire, promised them a Savior, and it still wasn't enough! Then once the Savior came, they tortured and killed Him. Now that's something to grumble about!

Instead, God left the grumbling to mortals. God, in His mighty and merciful love, saved us from our sins. Did you hear the Savior from the cross? He prayed! He asked God to forgive those who put Him there. He prayed for us.

The next time you arrive at school with a fresh grumble waiting to erupt, sit in one of your student's chairs (which might be cause for righteous grumbling!). Think of her needs, and pray for her. Then move to the next chair, and do the same. Continue until you've blanketed heaven with prayers for all your students. Be sure to thank God for them too.

Prayer

Thank You, Lord, for giving me a variety of students who have many needs. Help me to teach them in Your name. Stir in me love and gratitude rather than grumbling. Amen.

And Be Quiet

In case you haven't noticed, this meditation is a sequel to number 15. As was the case last time, we'll begin with a quotation. This is the prayer of a church member who will remain nameless in case you know him: "Use me, Lord, in Thy work—especially in an advisory capacity."

> I waited patiently for the LORD; He turned to me and heard my cry. ... Be still, and know that I am God; I will be exalted among the nations, I will be exalted in the earth.
>
> *Psalm 40:1; 46:10*

Then there is the prayer of a young boy urged by an angry teacher to pray. He said: "Lord, make me behave better, but if You can't do it, that's okay. I'm having a good time."

Have you acted on the suggestion at the end of the previous devotion? Have you noticed answers to your prayers (without looking at today's absentee list)? Have you thought about what results you expect from your conversations with God? Did He even hear you?

You've probably been praying long enough to know that God answers prayers in His own time and in ways far better than you can anticipate. You also may admit that sometimes God's answers are surprising—even a bit disappointing.

How much easier it would be if God just fixed the problem in His divine way and on a schedule convenient for you. The reality that prayer doesn't work that way was made clear in a dark garden late one night. It wasn't that the prayer lacked fervor. So anguished and impassioned was His prayer that blood sweated from His skin. He hoped His Father would find some easier way to accomplish the task that lay ahead of Him. But it wasn't to be. The Father told Him that only He could be the answer to this prayer. So Jesus suffered and died for our sins.

Back to your prayers. Sit in those students' chairs again, and take your Bible. This time be quiet. Let God talk to you. You prayed for the needs of your students; obviously, you know some of those needs. Could it be that God wants you to be the answer to your prayer? You may discover that He wrote the answer in the pages of His Journal.

Prayer

Please answer my prayers, heavenly Father. Give me strength to do what You ask of me. In all that I do, let me do it to Your glory. Amen.

17

Raise Your Hand

Early comedy movies often employed sight gags. One such gag was set in a military training camp. (The characters might have been the heavy half of Abbott and Costello or Curly of the Three Stooges.) All the soldiers lined up before the sergeant, who bellowed a call for volunteers to take one step forward. Everyone but the hapless victim took one step backward. The protesting "volunteer" was accepted by the sneering sergeant.

> Each one should use whatever gift he has received to serve others, faithfully administering God's grace in its various forms. *1 Peter 4:10*

If your school uses volunteers, you probably suffer from a national trend that reveals decreasing numbers of those willing to give their time. Too bad you can't pull an Abbott and Costello on them! But maybe you can. First, a little background to set the mood.

Remember the disciples? (Your students probably think you knew them personally!) They were an eager lot, though not always resourceful. As willing as they were to learn about salvation and to share that news with others, they sometimes lacked vision. Or maybe it was faith. Take the feeding of the multitude, for example. "Feed them? But where will we get the food?" the disciples asked. Maybe those words tumbled out with expectations that Jesus would whip up a feast from less than scratch. But Jesus had other plans. Eventually, the disciples learned to be good volunteers, going where there was need.

Sin sometimes makes us sit on our hands. We don't want to get involved. After all, we do enough already. Teaching full time leaves little desire to volunteer for more of the same on Sundays. And what about those long evening meetings for those who volunteer for other projects? We are too busy or too tired for that.

The Holy Spirit will help us overcome excuses and make us wave our hands as excitedly as a second-grader volunteering to erase the board. Even if you are busy, give some thought to how you might further serve—it doesn't have to be church-related. God asks Christians to work outside the church too. When you consider your vast experience as a Christian teacher, doesn't it seem that God made you for moments like these?

Prayer

Come, Holy Spirit, and raise my hands to volunteer. Send me wherever God needs another worker. Amen.

18

The Phone Rings

The marvels of modern telecommunications have increased the opportunities for parents to ruin your day beyond the phone call during dinner or first thing in the morning. Before the age of answering machines, voice mail, and fax machines, you could ignore the phone and postpone expected unpleasantries. Now some inventive genius needs to create ways to delay the inevitable.

> Repent, then, and turn to God, so that your sins may be wiped out, that times of refreshing may come from the Lord.
>
> *Acts 3:19*

Not to deny the legitimacy of some parental phone calls, but they sometimes seem a likely object lesson on the work of the devil in your life. Consider this scenario.

Ring. Ring. Ring. Ring. Ri—

"Hello, Jim Teacher speaking."

"Mr. Teacher, am I catching you at a bad time? Good. I have a few grievances ... er, concerns I need to air. Have you got some time? Good because I have an eternity, and that's probably too little time for a busy person like me.

"You need to spend more time planning your lessons. I saw you hitting baseballs at the park last Sunday when you should have been hitting the books. Six students in your class missed the point of the lesson because you didn't use the 'Extending the Lesson' section in the manual.

"And do you know how many people heard what you said when the orange juice carton fell out of the refrigerator? No one heard but me. And God. How about your TV viewing habits? I really enjoyed that program you watched last Tuesday.

"You know that student you dislike? He's my friend! But you're supposed to like everybody, right? That's what God and the principal say. Well, I could go on for hours, but I'll save it up for the next time I call. Talk to you in a few days!"

The devil has multiple personalities, and all of them are bad, even when they seem sweet. One of Satan's perverse pleasures is to accuse us, seeking to drive us to despair or to deflate the self-image Christ wants us to have. To make matters worse, the devil often is accurate in his accusations. What can you do?

Today's Bible passage has the answer. Nothing refreshes quite like the results of repentance. It cools down the devil too. Use it often to dampen his spirits.

Prayer

Lord Jesus, I sin often and need Your forgiveness. Refresh me with new life in You. Amen.

19

IEP

Consider the advantages of present-day schools:

- Students do better at geometry. They know all the angles.

But we ought always to thank God for you, brothers loved by the Lord, because from the beginning God chose you to be saved through the sanctifying work of the Spirit and through belief in the truth.

2 Thessalonians 2:13

- Preschoolers come to school knowing at least two letters of the alphabet—*T* and *V.*

- Students have access to reading specialists, occupational therapists, psychologists, and lawyers.

- Kids with special needs get individualized education.

Yes, one much-needed service is the IEP—a plan to help children learn by using their unique skills and compensating or otherwise addressing the obstacles that block learning. The IEP has done much to help children whose learning styles or abilities differ from the average student. Of course, many Christian schools practiced IEPs long before they became a popular educational concept. Another way to define an IEP is to call it "caring" for each child in the classroom. God invented a superb precedent for IEPs and applied it to all His children because they couldn't succeed by themselves.

God had an IEP for each of us. He knew precisely our needs, even before we were born. He designed a plan intended to bring nothing but good into our lives. But He also planned for contingencies, those times when sin would thwart the plan and threaten disaster. Knowing our sinful inclination to destroy our relationship with Him—and with ourselves—God planned a way to restore the relationship and save us. Because Jesus suffered and died to take away our sins, the divine IEP continues for us. God even provided a special tutor.

The Holy Spirit continues to implement God's IEP. He brings us along in just the right ways, delivering blessings as needed, seeing us through difficult times, helping us reject temptations, nudging us to repentance, and feeding us with Word and Sacrament.

Some of us, perhaps most of us, are slow learners, but the Spirit never grows impatient. He loves us. Besides, the Holy Spirit was with Jesus as He weathered temptations, so He knows the devil's power. The Holy Spirit also knows that we lack the personal resources to resist without divine intervention.

God has given us everything we need to succeed. To be honest, we owe our entire success to Him. Someday we'll graduate. Be sure to thank Him when you give your speech. (And quote today's Bible passage too!)

Prayer

Thank You, heavenly Father, for taking care of me. Praise to You for giving me everything I need for life here on earth and later in heaven. Amen.

20

Last Chance

A teacher in Wyoming reported that eight years ago she decided to procrastinate, but she never started. This proves that some things must be put off dozens of times before they completely evaporate from memory.

> The day of the Lord will come like a thief. The heavens will disappear with a roar; the elements will be destroyed by fire, and the earth and everything in it will be laid bare. *2 Peter 3:10*

Christian teachers can't afford to procrastinate. As today's Bible passage states, time is uncertain. Skeptics might ask why we are concerned with teaching a body of knowledge, particularly information about the Christian faith. After all, this knowledge will die with the individual—and the world—anyway. While that is certainly true of most knowledge and even of most religions, it is wrong about Christianity.

God has been patient with civilization. Many events of human history defiantly taunted Him to end the world. His love for creation, however, prompted timely delays—time for more people to hear His call. How many people will continue to enjoy this divinely beneficial procrastination? Will the end of the world find many cursing their own delays or suffering the eternal panic of being too late?

Do any children in your class not believe that Jesus saved them from sin? What about their families? Undoubtedly the Holy Spirit works mightily through your religion lessons, igniting faith in young souls. Undoubtedly the Spirit also works through your deeds, demonstrating the love of Jesus and prompting children to thirst for more. You may be the only one to tell a child about Jesus. By the power of the Holy Spirit, he may believe despite resistance from other family members. Who knows how long that child will remain in your care. Families have a habit of moving, and if this child doesn't hear about Jesus from you, he may never hear the Good News. You may be his last chance. You may be the family's last chance.

Sin may bring fear into your heart. "How will parents react when they learn what I have taught their child? Would it be better for the child if I didn't talk about my faith? I better think about this—I don't want to be too hasty." And the sin of spiritual procrastination rears its ugly rear. (Yes, *rear!*)

God chose you for the hard jobs such as working in the mission field known as your classroom. So put this book down and get busy. *Tempus fugit!* (I hope that means "Time flies." I always put off those Latin assignments.)

Prayer

Lord and Savior, thank You for giving me a divine mission. Help me overcome fear and other obstacles that prevent me from sharing the Gospel. Amen.

Routines

It's been said that a person who never makes mistakes is boring. (Oh, for a little boredom in the school office!) If the previous statement is true, perhaps it explains a lot about our relationship with God, at least from our perspective. God never enjoys blissful boredom with us sinners running rampant here on earth.

The LORD answered Moses, "Is the LORD's arm too short? You will now see whether or not what I say will come true for you." Numbers 11:23

In today's Bible passage, the Lord sounds peeved with Moses. It seems that Moses doubted God's intervention despite the many wonders he had witnessed. Perhaps God's displays of power had become so routine that Moses doubted it could get any better. What may be most accurate is that Moses was upset by current circumstances and shot off his mouth without thinking.

You are a routine Christian, living a routine Christian life. For many, this routine is beyond imagination—like poverty-stricken people in developing nations. And in some ways, we Christians are a lot like Moses and his lot.

The Bible says that God blesses believers and unbelievers alike, and we have ample evidence of it. Rain falls on the farms of both. Babies are born to both. The earth transports both around the sun in a regular, predictable pattern. These events are so common that even God's people are tempted to forget their miraculous nature. Of course, this is just what the devil desires, and we easily merge into his malevolent mind-set.

We combat this malaise when we confess our sin and hear God's forgiveness. And we know that the Holy Spirit is at work in our hearts to make us more aware of God's action in our lives, even in matters we consider ordinary.

Most humans fail to realize that boredom is often a blessing. It's a sign that God's conventional yet magnificent system of blessings works well. Sometimes it's good to be bored. It gives us time to relax and think about what God has done, and that's bound to add some genuine excitement to life!

Prayer

Thank You, Lord, for giving me a routinely blessed life. Help me never to doubt Your action in my life, even during those stable times when I am tempted to forget how You exercise Your divine power. Amen.

Confusion in the Classroom

An expert is
- someone who can create confusion from simplicity.
- someone who can take what you already know and make it confusing.
- someone who can multiply his own confusion by the number of people listening to him.

He saved us, not because of righteous things we had done, but because of His mercy. He saved us through the washing of rebirth and renewal by the Holy Spirit. Titus 3:5

At that rate, we have no need for experts in our classrooms, and you can be pleased if nobody has ever considered you one. Confusion is a virus in education. You probably have witnessed the effect of mass confusion if you ever have

- confused the fire alarm with the weather warning signal.
- tried to teach notes to nonmusical pupils.
- noticed you were wearing your watch upside down after you sent the kids to recess.

Confusion is downright deadly in spiritual matters, which makes teaching and living the faith both a special responsibility and a Godly privilege. God entrusted you with a serious matter. You are charged with the diffusion of confusion on matters related to faith, and you can assess all Christian teaching according to these simple elements: Law and Gospel.

Okay, so Law and Gospel aren't so simple. There's even an intensely detailed lecture series on the topic. (Surprisingly, the lectures are collected in a book entitled *Law and Gospel.*) It can be easy to confuse Law and Gospel or to ignore one or the other. Here's a refresher course: The Law tells us what we should do, thus revealing what we have done wrong. The Gospel tells us what God has done on our behalf.

Now you can analyze your teaching. There is, of course, need for both Law and Gospel in the classroom. Sometimes, however, religion lessons end with little Gospel—which is intended to comfort students when they sin—and lots of morality—which provides no comfort. Another danger, a serious one, is when we come to believe that we don't need the Gospel because we can and do obey the Law! The corollary of this danger is that we can focus entirely on the Gospel to the exclusion of the Law. Then our students may wonder why they need a Savior in the first place.

Avoid confusion in your classroom. Teach Law. Teach Gospel. But don't mix the two. It's worse than sulfuric acid and water!

Prayer

Keep us clear, dear Holy Spirit, on the difference between Law and Gospel as we teach children the Word You inspired. Amen.

Virtual Reality

Virtual reality is the rage these days. By ensconcing yourself in an electronic headdress and sealing the real world from view with special goggles, you can experience something that you're not really experiencing. You literally fool your senses.

Therefore, as God's chosen people, holy and dearly loved, clothe yourselves with compassion, kindness, humility, gentleness and patience.

Colossians 3:12

What if you could exile yourself to virtual reality and see both you and your classroom through the eyes of a student? First would come the typical groans emitted when you see yourself on videotape. You're too tall or too short, too fat or too thin, your hair doesn't match your shoes, your hair doesn't match anything because you have none, your voice is too squeaky, and ... Well, let's leave the humiliation at that.

Next would come other impressions of yourself—how much you smile or frown or look like a self-controlled poker player holding a big hand. You would hear the tone of your voice—friendly, demanding, encouraging, demeaning, warm, coldly objective. Then you would pick up the nonverbal signals—what your eyes do when you talk and listen, how you fold your arms or adjust your posture to various situations. In the end, you would see how you match the command of today's Bible verse. Yes, virtual reality would provide a realistic view of yourself.

Taking virtual reality one step further, think of what you would experience if you could see what God sees in you. (Go ahead. Think about it. Is the tissue box or blood pressure medication nearby?)

You may have imagined some horrible sights. It's easy to conjure up hues of hatred, columns of contempt, bushels of bad words, layers of lust ... and here we are back at humiliation again. Rightly so too. That was more than imagination. It was truth. But back to what God sees. Slip on the virtual reality helmet, and what do you really see? Close your eyes. That's what God sees. He sees nothing of what you saw. He sees Jesus, His precious Son, and His righteousness. Jesus took all your sin and humiliation to the cross—and left it there. In exchange, He has clothed you in Himself. God has nothing to hold against you. Maybe it's time to let students see you that way too.

Prayer

Lord Jesus, thank You for making me blameless before God. The virtual reality of the Gospel is better than virtual. It is absolute. I praise You for saving me. Help me share the reality of my salvation with others. Amen.

Imagination

Today's Bible passage suggests a creative art project, doesn't it? Picture it: a whole choir of pines swaying rhythmically, lifting graceful boughs toward heaven, breaking the silence of the forest with melodic praise to God.

> Then the trees of the forest will sing, they will sing for joy before the LORD, for He comes to judge the earth.
>
> *1 Chronicles 16:33*

Teachers marvel at the imagination of children. They marvel even more at parents whose imagination about their child's potential often exceeds the child's imagination! But young children dwarf us in the imagination field. They can play for hours, seeing in their minds what TV commercials often picture to make toys look better than they are. Imagination fuels the writer, the artist, the visionary, the daydreamer, and the lazy student who hopes to pass this year.

A sage once said that imagination is given to people to compensate for what they are; a sense of humor is given to console them for what they aren't. That's not really so sage, though. God has something better to give.

Jesus is not a product of our imagination. God gave us Jesus to compensate for what we are. Often, childhood imagination, especially among boys, conjures up heroes; yet the greatest hero is real. Jesus lived a perfect life to compensate for sinners who don't even come in a close second, even with a lot of imagination! He carried our sins to the cross, suffering unimaginably to remove the pain of eternal punishment and death from our future. Then Jesus rose from the grave, something beyond the imagination of even His closest followers. He will return to take us to heaven someday. That, too, will be more than our human minds can conceive.

We don't need humor to console us for what we aren't. But we can enjoy humor because God has eliminated the burden of saving ourselves. We are all too human, which is probably laughable but not in a truly joyful way. Our real consolation, which allows us to laugh and to enjoy life, is ours through faith. It soothes us, strokes us, and sometimes even tickles us with the joy of our salvation. Faith is so sure, so comprehensive, that it leaves nothing to our imagination.

Prayer

Thank You, God, for creating and maintaining me. Thank You, Jesus, for saving me. Thank You, Holy Spirit, for filling me with faith and truth. Thank You for leaving none of this to my imagination. Amen.

Mnemonic Phonics—A

Now it's your turn. Setting aside the philosophical and pedagogical battles over the place of phonics in the curriculum, it's your turn to receive some phonics lessons. We'll focus on the vowels. We will use the vowels as mnemonic devices—mental mechanisms to help us remember what God has done for sinners. Today we'll take the *A* sounds, like the one you probably muttered when you discovered you were taking phonics again.

A is for *agapé*. (Not to be confused phonically with *agape*, though *agapé* probably leaves us *agape* with pleasant surprise.) *Agapé* is the Greek word for the love Jesus has for us and the kind of love He desires us to have for each other. We often fall short of *agapé*, but Jesus has enough to cover that as well as a multitude of other sins.

A is also for the sound in *Father*. Sometimes it's a soothing sound, like the one you make when someone rubs your back.

Sometimes it's a sound of delightful discovery as in "Aah, you remembered my birthday!" When it comes to our loving God, it's always a capital sound!

A is for *absolute* as in Psalm 103:12. It describes the extent to which Jesus obliterated our sins. That's why *absolution* is such a good word to describe what the pastor does when he pronounces forgiveness. He absolutely absolves us from guilt, showing that through Jesus we are saved from eternal punishment *and* we have the gift of eternal life in God's presence. Absolutely wonderful!

A is for the sound in *fare* and *fair* as in "Jesus paid our full *fare* to heaven even though the price was not *fair* to Him."

A is for the sound of the second A in *always.* That's how often Jesus is with us. How terrible if He were only an occasional visitor or came only when invited! But He is always here. This comforts us as we live each minute of life in His care and under His love! He knows everything about us, even our most private sins. But that need not frighten us. He forgives. Always.

Prayer

Almighty Lord, thank You for making me a saved sinner. Stay with me always, and help me obey Your will. Amen.

Mnemonic Phonics—E

The sounds of *E* in its respective words also can help us remember God's goodness. *E* has only two basic sounds associated with it in this lesson. But they're good ones.

"I tell you the truth, whoever hears My word and believes Him who sent Me has eternal life and will not be condemned; he has crossed over from death to life." *John 5:24*

E is for the sound in *debt*. That's a word familiar to many people because they are often there—just think about your house or car or the week's groceries. We are certainly there when we calculate what we owe God. He requires a perfect life from those who want to be His chosen people. That being impossible, He sent His Son to pay what we owe. Through His suffering and death, Jesus paid the debt we created. Although He doesn't demand repayment, He does teach us to forgive others as we have been forgiven.

How difficult it can be to forgive! Even when we forgive, sometimes it's impossible to forget. Our bitterness can cloud forgiveness. Not so with God. When He forgives and forgets, it's for eternity.

E is for the beginning sound of words like *eternity* and *eternal*. It's impossible to imagine anything lasting past its warranty date. That's why manufacturers require us to pay for their guarantee on products they know won't last. Not so with God. He promises eternity, and He doesn't confine the guarantee to fine print. It's right in the open as we read in today's Bible reading.

Tennyson said that in time there is no present, while in eternity there is neither past nor future. This explanation is as good as any because it hints that eternity is an everlasting moment. What will that moment be like? Perhaps we can compare it to that moment when Mary recognized Jesus near the tomb. Her love, her adoration, her unparalleled joy bubbled over in a single, explosive moment as she recognized her risen Savior. We will have a moment like that too. And it will last a lifetime.

Prayer

Eternal God, I don't understand the concept of eternity, but I live in certain hope that I will spend it with You. Come soon, Lord. Amen.

Mnemonic Phonics—I

Are you ready for Mnemonic Phonics session 3, or would you rather commit yourself wholly to whole language? See how the vowel *I* can help you think of God's work in everyday life.

I is for the first sound in *inheritance*. Now there's a popular subject, though large inheritances can be taxing. And while smaller inheritances come in handy, there are too many ways to spend them. The best inheritance, however, is the one mentioned in today's Bible reading. *Inheritance* is a fitting word for what we receive from the Lord. It accurately reveals how we come to possess God's gift of salvation and eternal life.

Except in rare cases, people receive an inheritance only after a death. Sometimes an inheritance is left to an individual who has been especially kind to the deceased, but most often it's left to peo-

And you also were included in Christ when you heard the word of truth, the gospel of your salvation. Having believed, you were marked in Him with a seal, the promised Holy Spirit, who is a deposit guaranteeing our inheritance until the redemption of those who are God's possession—to the praise of His glory.

Ephesians 1:13–14

ple because of their status as family members. These family members did nothing special to deserve the gift, which was left in the spirit of familial love.

We have inherited salvation because the Holy Spirit made us part of God's family. Often, we are not good family members—we rebel, disobey, and show a lack of respect for our Father. Because of Jesus' actions on the cross, we remain in God's family. With the death of Jesus and sealed by His resurrection, we have an inheritance. It's just a matter of time until we move into the mansion.

I is also for the sound we hear when referring to ourselves. Teachers often place tremendous value on fostering self-esteem in students. That's good as long as the focus on "I" doesn't become distended into the *I* of *idolatry*. Just as the *I* sounds the same in each, it's easy for people to idolize themselves. The good news, however, is that healthy self-esteem is based on God's love for us. He loved us and sent His Son to save us; therefore, we can love ourselves. Better yet, we can love others, and, most of all, we can love God. God's love—the *Is* have it!

Prayer

Dear Jesus, thank You for naming me in Your will. Help me use my inheritance to spread the Good News of what You have done. Help me especially to witness to my students and their families. Amen.

Mnemonic Phonics—O

O is the champion of vowels. It has more sounds than any other. It makes you want to rise up and voice a long ooooooooo—the kind you hear at a fireworks show. Okay, maybe it's harder to get that excited about a vowel.

The Son is the radiance of God's glory and the exact representation of His being, sustaining all things by His powerful word. After He had provided purification for sins, He sat down at the right hand of the Majesty in heaven. *Hebrews 1:3*

O is for the initial sound of *omni,* and not coincidentally, the main idea in today's Bible passage. God is *omni*present, *omni*scient, *omni*potent, *omni*everything! What comfort we have because we trust that God knows all. What comfort we have because we trust that God remains in charge, in command of the world. The devil cannot take us from God, unless, of course, we want to go.

O is for the sound we hear in *taught.* Don't you just love that word? You were chosen to teach, and you were taught how to do it. Because you are a Christian teacher, the Word of God is taught in your classroom every day.

(If you're not allowed to teach such "subversion" in your school, you can teach by example!)

O is for the last sound in *foe*. Last sound indeed! The evil foe still plagues Christians. He waves sin in front of our eyes, ears, and all our senses. And we fall. We give in. We sin. But God limits the foe's power. We bring our sins to Jesus each day, and He forgives. One day, the foe will lose his power forever as he goes for a dip in his flame-filled swimming hole.

O also can sound like *noise*—the kind of festival sounds we'll hear as we're taken to heaven. And it can sound like *took*—as in "Jesus *took* away our sins." (Maybe He dumps them into that lake of fire!) *O* can sound like *toot*, one of the noises we'll hear as the trumpet sounds. And finally, *O* can sound like *out*. The joy of salvation is *out* of this world.

Prayer

O powerful God, thank You for using Your power in love. Thank You especially for defeating that most dangerous of foes, the devil. Help me to teach others about Your most merciful and gracious acts. Amen.

Mnemonic Phonics—U

The last of the regular vowels brings us a few more ways to relate everything in life to God's love. Christian teachers in Christian schools grow accustomed to integrating faith and Scripture into all subject areas. But they can go even farther. Perhaps you can involve your children in a "Letter of the Week" and encourage them to relate all their words to God.

Who has believed our message and to whom has the arm of the LORD been revealed?

Isaiah 53:1

Our last study includes a word with which we struggle. The devil likes to plant it in our hearts, and we reluctantly give in. But not for long. As Jesus forgives and the Holy Spirit strengthens, we return to faith—often stronger for the battle. So what is the word?

U is for the beginning sound in *unbelievable.* Now this word is a problem for those who believe, as today's Bible passage confirms. It's an even bigger problem for those who vainly profess faith. So let's examine both sides of *unbelievable.*

Unbelievable! The tone of voice is hard, clipped, stubbornly emphatic—the hard-hearted voice of Pharaoh before the last plague or the contemptuous mockery of the Pharisees before they drove Jesus to Calvary. It's the timbre of modern academic voices denying that Christ existed or the sniveling whine of less-educated people too proud to humble themselves before God. Maybe it's even the voice of a few students who believe more in morphing cartoon characters than they do in the One who knows, loves, and saves them. So, Christian teacher, what can you do about this problem?

Agree. That's right, agree. Say the word, no croon the word, intoning it like a baseball announcer describing a diving catch in the outfield. *Unbelievable!* Yes, God's love *is* unbelievable. You cannot describe it adequately or use human vocabulary to argue in its favor. Even believers cannot fathom completely its depth or breadth. It *is* unbelievable to think that God would take the form of a human so He could face our temptations, sacrifice His life for our sins, and rise again for our eternal victory. It is unbelievable that we are His saints while we are still sinners.

Don't argue with those who don't believe. You cannot convince them. Pray for them instead. Pray that the Holy Spirit will work through the messages of faith that people like you share.

Prayer

Thank You, Lord, for making the unbelievable believable. Always let me marvel as I remember the incredible things You have done for me. Amen.

And Sometimes Why

The previous meditation addressed unbelief, particularly as it occurs in others. But haven't you had occasion for doubt too? Maybe your doubting has little to do with the essential truth of salvation: that Jesus died to take away your sins. Your doubt may center on what the Holy Spirit is doing in you and through you. Sometimes you may ask, or at least think, "Why, Lord? Why am I here? I don't feel very successful, and observable results seem to confirm my failure. Why, Lord?"

Is your labor in vain? Hardly. Reread Paul's words to the Corinthians. You might want to cut them out and tape them someplace inconspicuous yet visible—a kind of first-aid kit for sagging spirits. While your labor is not wasted, God does not promise easy going for believers either. This may be more true for teachers. You will face "momen-

> Therefore we do not lose heart. Though outwardly we are wasting away, yet inwardly we are being renewed day by day. For our light and momentary troubles are achieving for us an eternal glory that far outweighs them all. So we fix our eyes not on what is seen, but on what is unseen. For what is seen is temporary, but what is unseen is eternal.
>
> *2 Corinthians 4:16–18*

tary troubles," and they might seem to last many, many moments. Paul calls them "light," an amazing statement from someone who suffered for proclaiming the Good News.

Sin likes to invite believers to pity parties. What a failure we feel because that first-grader we taught was not baptized before he moved away. How we dwell on that class of eighth-graders that dutifully met the requirements for confirmation, but couldn't be convinced to attend church once the festivities ended. Then there's that fourth-grader who mocks you while you teach religion. You told her parent, but she mocked you too! What a miserable failure you are because you can't get through to these people!

Look for the first-aid kit. Read Paul's words when you feel ineffective, ignored, or abused. Paul knew the feeling well. Jesus knew it even better. Rejoice that Jesus works through you. The success of your efforts belongs to Him. You never know. When that child is 64 and you're long gone, she may remember what you taught. That will be just another of many surprises you'll have in heaven.

Prayer

Don't let discouragement defeat my ministry, Lord. You have called me to work for You in my classroom. Therefore, work through me and let the Holy Spirit make it a success. Amen.

Cooperative Learning

If you're an "older" teacher, the only time you experienced cooperative learning in elementary school was during art class. Or recess. Maybe lunch, if you were lucky. Had you tried cooperative learning in other subjects, it would have resulted in severe disciplinary action. Today, cooperative learning is a legitimate educational strategy, and those who have successfully employed it have discovered its merits.

For we are God's fellow workers; you are God's field, God's building.

1 Corinthians 3:9

Cooperative learning has existed from the earliest time, even before the advent of formally trained educators. The first episode of cooperative learning, however, had no benefit for the students. Adam and Eve learned that cooperating with Satan, as opposed to God, had serious consequences. They were expelled! From that time forward, Adam and Eve's garden of learning grew weeds as well as fruit.

If society were truly wiser as well as older, it would have learned from Adam and Eve. In a way, it did. A bad way. It found increasingly 'new and improved" ways to sin! Before we shake a nagging finger at society, however, we need to remember that we are members of it. How often we cooperate with the devil—every sin proves our cooperation. Satan undoubtedly revels in his success with us, short-lived though it may be. With no cooperation on our part, God sent His Son to take away our sins. Now we have immediate access to forgiveness. Once again, this isn't a cooperative effort. Jesus did it all!

Today's Bible passage tells us what Jesus gained for us on the cross in addition to forgiveness. Now we work with Him. As in most cooperative learning applications, it's good to pair advanced students with those of lesser abilities. No guessing who the advanced One is here!

We work side by side with Jesus in our classrooms. Together we undertake a vital project: proclaiming the Gospel. He brings in the Holy Spirit as a resource person, and together we shower our students with God's love. We immerse them not only in worldly knowledge but in spiritual truth. Yes, we can even work cooperatively at recess or in gym class! Isn't that what He meant by calling us His "field and building"?

Prayer

Thank You, heavenly Father, for working with us. At times we're so slow and unimaginative! Forgive us, and equip us to work successfully with You. To You we give all glory. Amen.

The Gifted Program

Educators are increasingly interested in research on the brain. In the past, they mostly were interested in "driving the car" rather than understanding how it worked. As long as students worked according to their ability—that sometimes vague measure—teachers were as happy as a student teacher after the first spelling test. You may categorize yourself thusly, so perhaps you would benefit from the following brain research.

His divine power has given us everything we need for life and godliness through our knowledge of Him who called us by His own glory and goodness. *2 Peter 1:3*

1. An eminent neuropedagogue recently announced that the human body often makes up for a kernel-sized brain with a bucket-sized mouth.

2. Humans sometimes confuse an open mind with an absence of anything between the ears.

3. Modern brains often suffer chronic unemployment.

4. Although the tongue is only a few inches from the brain, the two often seem much farther apart.

5. Regardless of "brainpower," *all* students qualify for gifted programs. So do all teachers.

Those who remember limited cooperative learning experiences also may remember when the only gifted program was that the smarter students didn't work as hard as the rest of us. Today, parents want accelerated or enhanced programs for their children, claiming special needs for those dubbed "gifted." Reading today's Bible passage, we might agree on this need, but we need to change the definition of "gifted."

God provides for His children (including you). This good news suggests that you may be smarter than you think. The gift of faith—believing Jesus is your Savior—opens the whole world and all of life to you. You see the "normal" events of life through eyes of faith, which favorably affects your perception. The gift of forgiveness frees you to serve God. The gift of the Holy Spirit enables you to serve in the unique ministry of a Christian teacher, just as He also calls others to serve in other capacities.

You are, indeed, gifted. Now get into that classroom, open your present in front of your students, and share it with them. Shower students with the present of your presence!

Prayer

Thank You, dear Father, for gifting me with faith and salvation. Help me foster this giftedness in others as I teach Your children. Amen.

High Tech

Computers were admitted to classrooms in the late 1970s. (Okay, some of you had them in 1965!) The earliest models were keyboards attached by modem to a huge mainframe, which was operated by a university with lots of money and lots of dreamers. Next, computers freed themselves of the tethers that had hooked them to remote locations.

For every house is built by someone, but God is the builder of everything. *Hebrews 3:4*

They stored their information on audiocassettes that operated at the speed of a dirge, and RAM was rated in single digits. Computers, being masters of memory, grew quickly to include 5 ¼ floppy disks, 3 ½ diskettes, CD ROMs, zip disks, and whatever else has been discovered while this is being written! In fact, computers have progressed so quickly that they often dash into obsolescence before you finish paying for them.

Computers aren't the only technology that teachers have welcomed (or at least admitted) into their classrooms. You may have large-screen TVs, video disk players, or at least a filmstrip projector with a light that works. Technology provides you with tools for teaching.

Have you noticed how God finds ways to use modern inventions? It should not surprise you, though. All you have to do is look at what He did with a handful of dirt! God the Creator places at your disposal an ambitious array of devices to assist you in ministry. He has blessed inventors with creative ideas and equally equipped others to make those ideas a reality. It's up to you—and society in general—to define how to use these inventions.

From books, magazines, and videotapes to cable TV and the Internet, we have learned to misuse God's gifts. The same thing happened with atomic power, gunpowder, and even eggs. (If you can't figure out how to misuse eggs, ask an adolescent!) Whatever appears in the world is subject to sinful abuse.

God may not build computers and other technology, but He is responsible for their creation. (If He actually built them, you wouldn't need a service contract!) He has given technology to teachers to expand their students' base of knowledge and its application. Christian teachers, like you, probably have some ideas about how technology can give glory to God. Christian chat rooms on the Internet, communication with missionaries, global prayer chains—it's all possible through God's blessings and the ingenuity He gives to people.

Prayer

Thank You, Lord, for giving us so many tools to use for learning and teaching. Help us use those tools correctly to build and strengthen Your kingdom on earth. Amen.

How Is Your Appetite?

Question: How are children and stomachs alike?

Answer: Neither needs all you can afford to give them.

"Blessed are those who hunger and thirst for righteousness, for they will be filled."

Matthew 5:6

Americans are blessed with more food to eat than any other nation. If this is true, why do we also have more diets to keep ourselves from eating?

If you are privileged to undertake lunch duty at school or to supervise a youth party that serves food, conduct an informal survey. You will need gloves and a strong stomach—maybe even a net! Go through the garbage (or catch it as it sails by), and retrieve the uneaten or partially eaten food. Wow! The results will stagger you, and we're not even talking about the smell!

This raises the question, "How is your appetite?" The answer is Matthew 5:6 as it appears above. Christian teachers are hungry and thirsty. Only one thing can satisfy them. Jesus is the miracle diet of Christians! Only

Jesus provides the feast of forgiveness that results in the riches of righteousness and the nourishment for work in His kingdom.

We should be starving. Often sin dominates our appetite for life. We indulge freely and bloat with guilt. God puts us on a diet of His Law and His love. He also heaps huge helpings of grace on us, which tips the scale away from obesity of sin to fitness of soul. And what good is fitness of soul? It's good for the heart.

Those on a liberal diet of grace and righteousness readily notice the same thing lunchroom supervisors notice. Some kids don't have lunch. When that happens, supervisors share their own meal or encourage those with plenty to sacrifice a little. Nothing warms the heart of a hungry child more than someone willing to share. Nothing warms a starving soul like the Holy Spirit working through you.

Spiritual food comes conveniently packaged. You'll find it under brand names like Baptism, Holy Communion, and the Bible. When it comes to spiritual food, make a pig of yourself.

Prayer

Feed me, O Holy Spirit. Nourish me with forgiveness and the Word. Like that little boy in the crowd gathered to hear Jesus, give me enough to share. Amen.

Watch Your Step

How embarrassing! You are playing with the kids because you have decided that you're only as old as you feel. The ball comes your way. You perform the athletic maneuver known as "skid and plop." Since it is both visual and audible, two sensual stimuli bombard your unintended audience's *cortex humori.* Suddenly, you feel 103, and you are acting as old as you feel. Whatever happened to Psalm 66, anyway? So much for keeping "our feet from slipping"!

Praise our God, O peoples, let the sound of His praise be heard; He has preserved our lives and kept our feet from slipping. *Psalm 66:8–9*

Applied to physical conditions, Psalm 66 would reduce health insurance premiums significantly. Actually, it does better than that. It covers life itself. (Certain exclusions apply for those participating in risky behaviors such as not acting your age, issuing failing grades to all students, and attending a parent-teacher meeting with something unzipped!)

All manner of slippery things litter your path. The devil lays tons of banana peel perversions before you. He fully supports the ways your "sinful flesh" tries to trip you. In cases such as these, the "skid and plop" syndrome can have eternal consequences. But it's cases like these that are fully covered by God's insurance.

Insurance isn't helpful until something tragic happens. The same is true for your policy with God, rather God's policy with you. If you were perfect, you would never collect. Of course, that's a big "if." In fact, it's impossible to be perfect. Although you skid into sin and plop into iniquity, God picks you up. He supports you on one side with Jesus, who died to take away your sins, and on the other side with the Holy Spirit, who steadies you through Word and Sacrament.

God makes you spiritually sure-footed, regardless of your athletic ability. He also gives you the ability to tell others about this miraculous skill. Like most difficult ventures, skill is only part of learning; the other part is attitude. God provides that too, only He calls it faith. Share your skills with others, especially the young people you serve. Ask the Holy Spirit to make them as grace-full as you are.

Prayer

Thank You for picking me up when I fall, dear Lord. Keep the slippery things on my path from harming me. Fill me with Your grace and mercy and peace. Amen.

Titles

What do your students call you? Okay, what are they *supposed* to call you? How do you feel about your title? Have you earned it? Would you rather be called something else? How do you like the title suggested by today's Bible verse?

The Spirit Himself testifies with our spirit that we are God's children.

Romans 8:16

God's children can be any age. Isn't it strange, however, that sometimes the older God's children get, the less they like the title "child"? At what age did you want to shed the title? It usually happens when independence squirms out of its latent cocoon and views "child" as some inferior or incapable life-form. And there is some truth in that.

Christians exist at various levels of maturity, just like children. No Christian will mature completely on earth, so all Christians are children to some extent. Where are you on the spiritual time line?

You may be a very young Christian, despite your legal age. But don't fall into the trap of thinking legally; the Law is not usually your friend. It condemns you. It reveals your sins and weaknesses. But the Law also drives you to the cross where the Holy Spirit opens your eyes to see not a dying criminal, but a Savior dedicated to saving you. You see the Gospel. Now you know that a place awaits in the Savior's presence.

You may be a very mature Christian, but chronological age means little. You grew in faith through the means that God provided: Word and Sacrament. And you're still growing. You don't mind being called a child, especially a child of God. You have an innocence that comes from trusting God to care for all your needs.

Occasionally you resent being treated like a child. You want to tackle a few things by yourself, but you realize that you can't do anything well without God's help. And because of faith, you look forward to that day when your maturity becomes complete.

Most Christians are somewhere between the two extremes of "age." Is that where you are? Like anyone wavering between two poles of thought or action, you bounce back and forth. Because God loves you, He keeps you bouncing in His direction. It's like being at that "awkward" age! Yet He is your Father, and you are His child. You can't stay young forever, but you can never age too quickly.

Prayer

Make me mature in my faith, Lord Jesus. Thank You for bringing me up in faith and trust in You. Help me grow ever further into childhood. Amen.

37

Off the Subject

Admit it. It happens. Admit more. Sometimes it's fun! Educationally, we can attempt to give it some dignity. Maybe we call it spontaneous learning or a teachable moment. Often it's simply getting off the subject that we intended to teach. Everyone from preschool teachers to youth directors to adult Bible class instructors is susceptible. College professors fall prey to it too. Occasionally getting off the subject is more useful than sticking to the prescribed lesson plan. Sometimes it's a delightful diversion. At other times, it becomes detrimental. In its worst case, it fits the description of today's Bible passage.

> For the time will come when men will not put up with sound doctrine. Instead, to suit their own desires, they will gather around them a great number of teachers to say what their itching ears want to hear.
>
> *2 Timothy 4:3*

What distracts you most? Usually anything sinful will do. Regardless of how clean we keep our "ears" by hearing God's Word, Satan finds ways to make them itch. This or that temptation can appear rather enjoyable—or at least worth pursuing—when we are feeling lonely or bored or angry or sad. Of course, the devil also gets us "off the subject" when we feel confident or self-sufficient or guilt-free. There are so many ways to distract us! So many itches on our ears! So many people willing to change the subject as long as it has nothing to do with sin or salvation!

Eventually itching ears become hurting ears. Like most pain, it drives us to someone who can heal the hurt. There are many quacks waiting to bilk us. The only genuine healing comes from Jesus. You can identify Him easily. He is the only One who prefers to tell you what He has done. He asks you to give up things that harm you, and He will never require things that are not good for you. He never runs out of the medicine you need.

One thing about Jesus—He never gets off the subject. You can't distract Him with wickedness or with self-righteous claims of worthiness. He knows you're a sinner. That's why He came with such single-mindedness to win your forgiveness. He gets you from the subject of sin directly to the subject of salvation. With Jesus, there is no other subject.

Prayer

Dear Savior, keep me focused on You. Never let me wander, and help me to keep my students' full attention on Your love and mercy. Amen.

38

They'll Laugh at Me

If a child said, "I don't want to tap dance at the talent show. They'll laugh at me." what would you do?

> So do not be ashamed to testify about our Lord, or ashamed of me His prisoner. But join with me in suffering for the gospel, by the power of God.
>
> *2 Timothy 1:8*

a. Agree

b. Counsel: "There is nothing to be afraid of. Everybody does weird things."

c. Describe how you conquered fear to do a zither solo at your elementary school talent show.

d. Quote a Bible passage. (Ecclesiastes 3:4 might be one suggestion.)

What if the statement is: "I'm fearful of talking about Jesus. They'll laugh at me." Now the situation is more serious, and there is no way of tap dancing around an answer. Teaching in a Christian school often reduces the anxiety and other obstacles that can stymie witnessing. You are expected to witness—that's what happens in a Christian school. Yet within those four walls, ridicule may rise to the occasion. It's acceptable to witness during religion class or faculty devotions, but step beyond those boundaries and people may think your witness is oddly out of place. How do you respond?

First, agree. Some will laugh at you. There will be that student who thinks you're just "being a teacher" and the colleague that suspects you're a "radical." Then you might see that parent snickering because you're doing that wimpy "Christian" thing. Once you accept that others may find your behavior (and you!) strange, it reduces the anxiety. After all, active Christians are a bit "weird" when you think about it.

Second, discuss your uneasiness with other "weird" colleagues. Together, you may find mutual support as you share stories. Talk frankly with your students too. Older students may be openly receptive to such discussions They often have personal experience with the fear of witnessing. If nothing else, they will recognize you as being more human than they thought. (Now there's something to laugh about.)

Third, quote a Bible passage. Today's selection is a good choice. "But join me in suffering" may not be comforting, but it is realistic. Sort of like tap dancing your finest performance—right off the edge of the stage.

Prayer

O, Comforter, bring me the peace that comes from trusting in Jesus. Help me to witness despite my anxiety and the resistance of others. Amen.

Remedial Religion

Forgiveness is a popular subject, especially among those who need it. It's even more highly regarded among those who want it. All Christians—including you—fall into both categories.

Then I will teach transgressors Your ways, and sinners will turn back to You. Psalm 51:13

Jesus told His disciples to forgive the proverbial 490 times when others sinned against them. Of course, this didn't mean that we should add a notch to our Bibles every time we forgive someone, but it does provide a clear message about forgiving as one has been forgiven. When it comes to forgiveness, even Christians sit in a remedial class.

How often do you need forgiveness? If the answer came quickly, it's probably correct. If you had to think about it, you are, if you'll forgive the expression, a little slow. Feelings of guilt are a sign of God's Law at work in your heart. They're more than feelings, though, they are truth! If you need more than the allotted time for silent confession during worship services, you know yourself well. The

Law is one way that God teaches us His ways, and our learning can be painful.

Because we often find ourselves in confession is proof that we are involved in remedial religion. Thank God that He's equally involved in forgiving. When we confess our sins, we simply agree with God that we are sinners, specifically recognizing certain behaviors—or lack of them—as acts outside of God's will. God hears our confession. Then He acts!

The imaginary gods created in the minds of heathens were gods of action too. Cross them and their wrath wreaked havoc. Though our God was angry over our sins, His love sent Jesus to the cross to wreak havoc on Satan. God's action saved us. We may be remedial learners, but there is nothing remedial about Jesus' work at Calvary. He did everything necessary to save us. Once. And for all.

Prayer

Thank You, dear Jesus, for taking away my sins. Although I rely on Your repeated forgiveness, give me power to sin less. Amen.

40

Persecution Complex

Persecution is no imaginary complex. If you lived in certain Muslim areas of the world, you could not read this book in public without risking your life. If you worked in a remote mission field, you could find yourself a maligned intruder in another culture's treasured way of voodoo life. Of course, you could experience the same conditions on the streets of Miami! (Okay, Floridians, many other places too.)

North American Christians have largely enjoyed their religious lives exempt from persecution. Or have we? Persecution at the point of a spear, the edge of a sword, or the end of a rope is easy to recognize. But we may face a more life-threatening persecution than we recognize. Subtle persecution is especially deadly.

> "Blessed are those who are persecuted because of righteousness, for theirs is the kingdom of heaven. Blessed are you when people insult you, persecute you and falsely say all kinds of evil against you because of Me. Rejoice and be glad, because great is your reward in heaven, for in the same way they persecuted the prophets who were before you."
>
> *Matthew 5:10–12*

Sticks and stones will break your bones, but words will break your soul. What kind of persecution sneaks up with little resistance to infect you? Subtle persecution starts with mockery of faith. At first, the jibes of those who recognize your Christian lifestyle may hurt you or make you angry. Maybe you'll respond by demonstrating your faith more boldly. Maybe you'll want to back off, avoid the line of fire. Maybe you'll keep quiet or show your persecutors that you can be part of the crowd. When that happens, persecution has succeeded as well as a slit throat, only its outcome is less messy.

Today's Bible reading blesses you as you live in the throes of persecution. Some verses tell you to expect persecution. Other verses emphasize forgiveness if persecution momentarily places you in denial of your Lord. (Peter had a good story about that.) Teach your students all these passages. Warn them about the persecution they will suffer as Christians. (Sometimes Satan even persecutes Christians by suggesting that life as a Christian is always bright and rosy.) Remember where to look for your reward. It will help you stand boldly against both sword and leer.

Prayer

Heavenly Father, give me insight that I may recognize persecution and stand against it, even when my physical life is not in danger. Send Your Spirit to protect my soul and the souls of my students. Amen.

Acting Like Kids

Oh, to be a child again! Would you welcome it, or are you content where you are? For some, childhood is an age. For others, it's a state of mind. Though you can't reduce the double digits of your age, you still may be a child at heart if the following describes you:

And He said: "I tell you the truth, unless you change and become like little children, you will never enter the kingdom of heaven." *Matthew 18:3*

1. You ask questions no reasonable person can answer.

2. You switch to the Cartoon Channel when nobody is looking.

3. You are still growing.

4. You act like a child despite your parents' best efforts to teach you better manners.

5. You enjoy singing "Jesus Loves Me."

The last on the list shall be first. Among the blessings of teaching children are the constant reminders of simple faith. Simple? Theologians have attempted to define and describe "faith" in detail. One oft-quoted scholar summarized faith most appropriately when he said, "Faith is believing what you know ain't so" (Anonymous). How interesting that people don't begin to think it "ain't so" until their childhood begins to seep away. In that light, Jesus' statement in today's passage makes lifesaving sense.

It is one of God's greatest miracles that the Holy Spirit plants faith in babies well before they can understand what Jesus did for them. Think of those faithful people who lose their memories because of age or accident. Their faith remains alive even as brain cells wither or malfunction. Add to your gratitude for the breadth of God's mercy those whose bodies age beyond the development of their intelligence. They also live with the gift of faith. In the end, they will have a superior life in heaven while those with tremendous intellect who "can't make sense" of faith will spend eternity in hell.

Don't ever become too smart! The faith you received by the power of the Holy Spirit is all you need. Your preschool faith grew enough to state the mystery in these poetic, profound, simple words: "Jesus loves me, this I know"! Through subsequent Bible study, the Holy Spirit led you to believe even more complex, unbelievable things—angels, the parting of the Red Sea, the virgin birth, and Christ's defeat of sin and death. Believing that these things are true fills an ever-growing storehouse of faith.

May your inner child always cling to the most elementary yet incredible truth: Jesus loves you.

Prayer

Thank You, Lord Jesus, for loving me even though I am unlovable. Thank You for making possible the miracle of faith that Your Spirit works in my heart and soul. Amen.

Results Count

Results count. Take Paul for example. Isn't it remarkable how much territory he covered and what he accomplished without owning a car? Then there are those whose only personal achievement is having dandruff. And even that gets washed away!

> Be patient, then, brothers, until the Lord's coming. See how the farmer waits for the land to yield its valuable crop and how patient he is for the autumn and spring rains.
>
> *James 5:7*

It's the same in school. First, the principal demands results, then parents demand even more. Second, you want results to bear witness that your dedicated work has accomplished something other than fattening a few slow-moving brain cells. Third, most children want results from their work. Finally, there's the local press, whose enthusiasm for reporting test scores is inversely proportional to the eminence of those scores.

God demands results. He made His expectations perfectly clear, even for muddled minds. His directive was simple: "Be perfect. Obey all I have commanded, and we'll get along just fine—you, Me, and the rest of the world." It didn't take long before the world's first inhabitants had some problems with that edict—it took only two chapters of the Bible, in fact. By chapter 3, we read of the first expulsion. The situation has worsened since then, and we find ourselves part of the problem.

Our best achievements fall short of God's minimum expectations. In short, we do not and cannot produce the results to satisfy God. Hang on—God found someone to produce the results for us. Not only did Jesus do everything necessary to achieve salvation on our behalf, but His work also empowered us to please God with our work. Now the things we do, once assessed as filthy rags, are works of art, or rather, works of Jesus!

What do you want from your class? You would like to see results from your lessons about Jesus' love and God's will. You don't need a tongue of fire dancing above their heads, but a puff of smoke would be appreciated. Be patient. Read today's passage. God has been patient with you, and look at the results. Point your students to Jesus, and let them know He's got results for them when they fail. And remember it yourself.

Prayer

Thank You, dear Savior, for doing the job God originally expected of me and my students. Now equip us to work for You, knowing that through our work, You will get more results. Amen.

Open-Door Policy

Some school administrators maintain an open-door policy, especially if you are in the office already!

Therefore, since we have been justified through faith, we have peace with God through our Lord Jesus Christ, through whom we have gained access by faith into this grace in which we now stand. And we rejoice in the hope of the glory of God. Romans 5:1–2

Satan maintains an open-door policy too. He's always accessible, though he frequently leaves his office vacant while he's out drumming up more business. That's not a problem, though. You can go right in and even sit in his chair. He wants you to feel at home. He welcomes sinners and is especially happy when he gets the ones that usually do business with his main competitor. Yes, Christians are always welcome in hell.

Sin would love to slam shut the door on us once we're inside. But thanks to God's mercy, Jesus has a foot in the doorway—not so we can enter, of course, but so we can escape the trap. That foot, if you look closely, has a strange mark on it. Bunions? Corns? Blisters? No, it's a scar where a nail once pierced it.

There are matching marks on Jesus' hands. Ugly? Yes. But they symbolize our salvation.

Jesus Christ brought an open-door policy to the world. It's a policy that makes God easily accessible to us. Oh, our respect and awe of Him probably would prevent us from even rubbing a thigh against His chair. That throne can belong only to One. But He probably would welcome us onto His lap! After all, He invites us to call Him Father. And His open-door policy ushers us to a new life.

The portal to new life is something that we eagerly aspire to *after* death. Yet God's door is open even in this temporal life. He welcomes repeated visits as we seek forgiveness. He gives us tools to fight temptation and cultivate grace. He even makes us part of His open door.

The Holy Spirit has chosen and equipped you to be a doorway to Jesus. Through the power of the Spirit, you open the gates whereby children enter God's new garden of paradise as you share God's Word. What children find through the portals of your Christian love are joy, peace, growth, and an immortal place in God's presence. No matter how your students behave or how successful they are, remember that you are a door. Keep it open.

Prayer

Use me, Holy Spirit, as an entrance by which my students can experience God's love through Jesus Christ. Amen.

44

Review Work

I will remember the deeds of the LORD; yes, I will remember Your miracles of long ago.

Psalm 77:11

Do you have kids start the day with a journal entry? You may invite students to share their journals so you can respond to their needs and concerns. Journaling is a relatively recent classroom tactic. It helps children express themselves. Journaling clears the mind and enables children to learn new ideas and experience fresh insights, such as how the stars stay in the sky, why farmers rotate crops, how to resist drugs, evidence of God's love among us, and how to avoid run-on sentences.

Teachers in some Christian settings, probably motivated by today's Bible passage, ask students to keep a Joy Journal. The children record at least one good thing that happened to them in the previous 24-hour period. (*Note*: If you try this with older students, don't be shocked if Monday morning's journal entry reads, "I didn't have to write in my journal yesterday." Sometimes blessings aren't what we expect.) When the exercise first begins, students sometimes have trouble remembering delightful deeds done for them. As they experience looking for the good in their lives, journal entries become easier to compose.

What joys characterize your teaching ministry? Do you talk about them as you gather with colleagues in the morning or at faculty meetings? Does your joy persist despite bad things? (Or is it rooted in worldly circumstances?)

One thing is certain: The joy of salvation (as we remember all God does and has done for us) is not a pair of parentheses in our lives. His miraculous deeds, especially the ones He did on the cross and in the cemetery, poured a foundation of happiness for us to enjoy and spread. (How could we laugh if it weren't for Easter?)

Good students anticipate what will happen next, so do good teachers. It should come as no surprise, then, that this meditation encourages you to keep your own Joy Journal. Record anything that brings you happiness. Then when you have a bad hair (bad nose, bad ear, bad neck, bad back ...) day, remember the root of all joy and use His name in your book.

Prayer

Lord of joy, thank You for bringing happiness to my life. Help me recognize ever more clearly my blessings from You. Amen.

45

Finders Keepers

Today's title was Tommy's favorite phrase. He chanted it and also appended the proper refrain: "Losers weepers." Nobody argued with Tommy or questioned his ethics. He was bigger than everyone else. Besides, whatever he found, he needed, especially money. His family was hard-working yet poor. They lived in a clean but sagging old house where a wheezing uncle was confined to the basement because he scared the neighbors. Yes, Tommy was a finder and a keeper. May God have blessed His life with finding and keeping spiritual treasures too!

> Philip found Nathanael and told him, "We have found the one Moses wrote about in the Law, and about whom the prophets also wrote— Jesus of Nazareth, the son of Joseph."
>
> *John 1:45*

Maybe you have a Tommy in your class. Maybe he sits at your desk. (Even if he doesn't have an intimidating uncle!) As Philip explained his "find" in today's passage, you probably related to the experience. You have found Jesus. Now you're going to keep Him!

Like Tommy, you identified yourself among the needy Eager to find relief from the impoverishment of guilt, you greedily searched for something to improve your condition. But nothing was to be found. Whatever was "out there" holding promise was little more than a penny when you needed thousands of dollars. Then, through the eyes of faith, you spotted your salvation, and you've been rich ever since. And you intend to stay that way! Then sin has its say. It wants you to lose what you have. Occasionally that happens. Thank God the condition is only temporary! Jesus turns our tears of sorrow into grins of grace. Finders keepers!

The truth, of course, is that you really didn't find Jesus. He found you. He came to you while you were still a sinner. Despite the misery you caused Him as He slumped with pain on the cross, Jesus loved you. He found you in need of Him, and He did something about it. Now He intends to keep you!

Prayer

Thank You for finding me, dear Jesus. I know I'm only one in a crowd of those who need You so I also thank You for finding others. You have found the children I teach too. They are dear to my heart, so I can only imagine what they mean to You. Keep them always. Amen.

Star of the Week

Modern people seem fascinated with stars. If they aren't worried about one falling from the sky, they are gazing intently toward them, hoping for signs of the future. Maybe it's not quite as prevalent today as it was in the 1960s. Back then "What's your sign?" was a common greeting. Of course, astrology persists in popularity. So do Hollywood and sports arenas—other sources of stardumb (pardon the sic joke).

> Those who are wise will shine like the brightness of the heavens, and those who lead many to righteousness, like the stars for ever and ever.
>
> *Daniel 12:3*

Kids like to be stars. They enjoy the attention, as do their highly paid counterparts in the adult world. Maybe you have tried a Star of the Week program in your classroom. The Star of the Week receives certain privileges, such as bringing his pet to school (as long as it's too small to swallow classmates whole). She can bring Mom and Dad to visit the class (usually less exciting than the pet). He might wear a crown or special hat so other students know he's the star. (*Note*: Do not attempt this above second grade!) She ends the week feeling better about herself, knowing that people recognize how truly worthwhile she is.

Daniel talked about stars. He talked about you. After all, haven't you led "many to righteousness"? Your class looks to you for leadership. They also expect wisdom, and as God's spokesperson to your classroom, you share His truth. As Daniel said on behalf of God, you shine like the heavens—a bright star speaking the eternal words of truth But before you fall into a black hole, you need to remember the source of your light.

Jesus was a star too. Thanks to Him, your future is no dark mystery. Jesus was the Star of the Weak. Through His death and resurrection, He saved you and the whole world. Your gifts of righteousness and Gospel-light illuminate a dark world or, at the very least, your classroom. So glow brightly, and lead your children on a trip through the stars.

Prayer

Dear Jesus, thank You for showing me the future. Thank You for making me and all Christians stars in Your universe. Grant me wisdom as I share my faith with students, and make me shine with Your Light. Amen.

Real Religion Never Rests

This book quoted her before. It would be interesting to meet the scholar affectionately known as Anonymous who said this about Christianity: "The religion of Jesus begins with the verb 'follow' and ends with the word 'go.'" Fits the title of this meditation nicely, doesn't it? James had a grasp of it, too, as today's Bible passage suggests.

> What good is it, my brothers, if a man claims to have faith but has no deeds? Can such faith save him? ... In the same way, faith by itself, if it is not accompanied by action, is dead.
>
> *James 2:14, 17*

Life as a Christian will never be comfortable. Because we have God's grace and His abundant blessings, we may be tempted to enjoy life with full confidence in the future. It is a sterile faith indeed that refuses to act in response to what God has done. James would say that faith without action is worse than sterile. It simply doesn't exist. He would appreciate Benjamin Disraeli's description of a faithful man: "His Christianity was muscular."

You likely have discovered the truth of the maxim "Real religion never rests." It began, of course, with Jesus. Had God's Son simply been someone passing Himself off as some god's son, the situation would be different. His followers would recline in temples with names such as La-Z-Boy or Beautyrest. But the true God's Son was an active person. His last three years were especially frenetic as He traveled constantly, teaching and healing everywhere He went. One of Jesus' few recorded moments of rest (in the boat on the Sea of Galilee) was interrupted by His disciples' frantic cries for help. Later, Jesus told His followers to "Go!" and they, too, proclaimed the Gospel, rarely resting. Many of them even died at work.

The ministry of Christ's first followers was one of muscle. You probably can identify with that as you conduct the ministry where He wanted you to go. You may serve first-graders or middle-school students rather than orphans and widows. However your work is no less important, and God will bless it. So make a muscle in the mirror every day. You'll probably notice it getting larger as the Spirit continues to bless you.

Prayer

Make me strong to do Your work, dear Jesus. I truly appreciate the rest You give, as well as the peace. Never let me abuse those gifts. Instead, send me into the world—or at least my classroom—to practice the faith You gave me. Amen.

The Handbook

The results of a survey conducted among a random sample of two principals indicated that at least one teacher on every staff knows the school handbook better than the principal. This often causes tension, especially on occasions when the principal would rather remain ignorant of what the handbook says. (Another random sample of teachers at the same two schools suggested that the principal succeeded in his quest for ignorance!)

> And now, O Israel, what does the LORD your God ask of you but to fear the LORD your God, to walk in all His ways, to love Him, to serve the LORD your God with all your heart and with all your soul.
>
> *Deuteronomy 10:12*

How many pages does your school handbook have? Typically, the older the school (or the administrator), the longer the handbook. Many school staffs prefer as few rules as necessary. Unfortunately, new rules become necessary every time somebody finds a new way to do something wrong. Wouldn't it be nice if just a few general rules would cover everything? While some schools accomplish that, general rules covering expectations become subject to interpretation or, more likely, misinterpretation. So? More rules!

The Bible is filled with rules, especially the Old Testament. Leviticus, for example, gives federal law some real competition for breadth and depth. None of these rules would be necessary if God's people (including us) could and would comply with today's Bible passage. Of the four parts of the verse, we might do well with one or two for about a second, but perfect obedience is completely impossible. Such is the life of sinners like us. We know the rules, but we can't obey them. And the devil is always there to remind God of what we're doing to His rules!

Good thing Jesus took care of this problem. Instead of creating more rules that would further bury us in noncompliance, Jesus obeyed the ones already in place. And He did it for us! Then, to simplify things, He focused the rules on two tasks: Love God. Love people. Easy, huh?

Complete obedience remains impossible. To correct the problem, we have complete forgiveness. Thanks to Jesus who replaced the handbook with the Book of Life.

Prayer

Thank You, heavenly Father, for letting me know what You expect. Grant me the will and ability to obey You, and forgive me when I fail. Amen.

The Sweet Smell of Success

Sometimes you don't realize the importance of your service. Someone (probably Anonymous again) said, "Service is nothing but love in work clothes." Then there's an Irish proverb: "God likes help when helping people." Being a servant, you probably could coin a few phrases yourself. Then again, those accustomed to service often forget that what they do really is a service.

"When she poured this perfume on My body, she did it to prepare Me for burial." Matthew 26:12

You serve your students and their families. Others probably don't understand how you feel about being a servant. It's not a popular career choice. Of course, servanthood has some perks that were absent in ancient times, a salary being a prime example. How blessed you are to serve others *and* to get paid for it! Surely, you are a success.

Success smells, but it isn't always sweet. Those you serve sometimes make it hard for you to succeed, and that stinks. Perhaps it's that model family that suddenly disintegrates because Dad gets caught in an affair. The children end up afraid, confused, and prone to hostility. Or maybe it's that single mom whom you convinced to attend church, but now you detect whiskey on her breath when she brings Sarah to school. Or it could be your school's governing body, which refuses to grant raises but wants you to teach a Tuesday evening Bible class. And maybe it's yourself as you neglect your family in the name of service to others. Sin exposes success at servanthood to rot and mold.

Only God makes the smell of success sweet. Successful acts of service need not be dramatic nor confined to limited situations. Consider today's Bible passage. Death is hardly ever associated with sweet smells. But Jesus' death is different because it spelled sweet success for sinners. In today's Bible passage, Jesus considered the woman's service as genuine perfume to Him, though others certainly questioned it. Jesus judged by His standards, though. Things done in service to God are worthwhile—and successful. So add a little cologne to your service. The aroma is sure to cover those areas that otherwise would reek with the stench of sin.

Prayer

Thank You, Lord, for making me a servant. Equip me to remain a servant, especially to young people and their families. Accept the perfume of my service to Your glory. Amen.

Estimated Worth

Parents appreciate you, especially on rainy Saturdays or long summer days! You need not fear replacement by a machine either. Who could automate blowing noses and removing snowsuits and boots? You deserve a lot of credit, and on your salary, you probably need it! Okay, okay. Enough of these backhanded compliments. The best that can be said to you is what Paul said to the Thessalonians in today's Bible verse.

> For what is our hope, our joy, or the crown in which we will glory in the presence of our Lord Jesus when He comes? Is it not you? Indeed, you are our glory and joy.
>
> *1 Thessalonians 2:19–20*

Glory and joy—words that characterize you and the contribution you make to the Church. Notice the capital *C*? It's also true for the church with the lowercase *c*. As one who does more than teach facts and subjects, your real value lies in the total ministry you provide: words, deeds, and actions. Regardless of your salary, your estimated worth extends beyond wallets and purses. You teach children about Jesus, then you show them what He is like.

As good as you are, you're probably not in danger of rising above humility. You know your weaknesses, faults, and sinfulness even better than those who call you during dinner or on Sunday afternoons. The actual value of a Christian teacher's ministry is not ted to your goodness. It's connected to God's goodness through Jesus' actions for you.

You haven't come this far by yourself. It was God Himself who first spotted you. He knew you before you were born, and He chose you to work for Him. Along the way, you had family, friends, pastors, or teachers who nourished your faith and encouraged you. Once you became a teacher, things might have changed. Support may be less than you would like, but that is a common experience for most teachers. You can remain confident, however, that God blesses your work. That's the ultimate in appreciation.

Someday you will meet Paul. You can quote 1 Thessalonians 2:19–20 when you do. He probably will return the compliment.

Prayer

Dear Jesus, thank You for the gift of salvation. Dear Father, thank You for planning my future even before I was born. Dear Holy Spirit, make me a good teacher—one who brings joy and glory to God. Amen.

Bulletin Bored

The sign in front of a small Christian school in a rural Idaho town proclaims "Home of the Legends." Maybe the "legends" are the 1938 State Champion choir or Mr. Hotentottle, who is celebrating his 83rd anniversary in the teaching ministry. Most of the school's graduates, however, know the real legend. It's the sixth-grade bulletin board that hasn't changed since cork was discovered!

> The Law was added so that the trespass might increase. But where sin increased, grace increased all the more.
>
> *Romans 5:20*

Perhaps you've discovered the secret of bulletin boards. They may not go away, even if you ignore them, but they will fade from consciousness. (Until a 30th reunion when several alumni discover their artwork has been immortalized. Or was it fossilized?) On the positive side, students entering the classroom for the first time will not suffer the same boredom as those leaving after a year. So allowing displays to "age" isn't completely unconscionable.

Bulletin boards are a lot like sin and grace. Both persist and abound to degrees that are likely to bore us. That's dangerous!

Take sin, for example. You probably do—regularly. Some sins slam into your conscience, shocking you into immediate repentance. These are the sins you never thought *you* would commit. You not only offended God, you disgusted yourself. Of course, there are also the more common sins—the ones at the fringe of consciousness because of their redundancy, the ones that hunker down in the shadows of your conscience. Maybe you've adopted several of these as pets because Satan thought you could give them a good home.

You are familiar with God's grace through Jesus too. As today's Bible passage says, it's around as much as your sins. Forgiveness shares some similarities with sin. There is the forgiveness that relieves us in the most noticeable ways—the kind we feel after one of those shocking sins. Then there is the more common variety, the kind you ask for in your "generic" repentance mode when you lump all your sins into a single "forgive us our trespasses."

It's a good thing God's forgiveness is so reliable. Not that you have license to abuse it or take it lightly. Forgiveness cost Jesus His life, and there's nothing legendary about that. It's 100 percent fact! Praise God for sending Jesus to take away your sins. It was no little thing—your sins *or* His mercy.

Prayer

Lord Jesus, let me never be so bored with my sins or Your forgiveness that I forget the realities of my life and the extent of Your love. Amen.

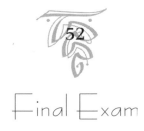

Final Exam

You have completed *Teaching 101*. When you complete something in school, it's time to examine yourself. It's time for the dreaded final exam.

> Examine yourselves to see whether you are in the faith; test yourselves. Do you not realize that Christ Jesus is in you?
>
> *2 Corinthians 13:5*

The second sentence makes this sound like a lenient test. Examine yourself? What student wouldn't tingle with delight at that prospect? On the other hand, maybe it's more difficult than it sounds. Self-examination can take two courses. There's the easy way: one question, true or false. Of course when you think it's a cinch to ace the test, sooner or later the problems come. Sooner—when you realize you're fooling yourself. And later—when you are expected to apply what you know.

The second course for this self-examination is equally as bad. When you look at yourself, you might be an extra-critical judge. No matter what you know, how well you know it, what you can do, or how well you can do it, it's never enough to satisfy you.

Having examined the phrase "examine yourself" and finding the process more difficult than it appears, let's see what Paul wanted to assess. He wanted to "see whether you are in the faith." Sounds serious, doesn't it? In fact, your life depends on your answer.

What's the best way to examine yourself for faith? If you examine yourself according to the first course, the answer is an automatic yes, no further thought necessary. But what about those late-night nagging doubts? Taking the second course might find you comparing and contrasting the good you have done with the bad you have done divided by all the things you should have done but didn't do. The answer might prod you to try harder, but the harder you try, the more you perceive your deficiencies. Woe is you!

Paul, being the good teacher he was, would sympathize with your dilemma. In fact, he shamelessly recorded his own examination in Romans 7. But in Romans 5:1–2, Paul answered the question of whether you are in faith. Here's the answer word for Word: "Therefore, since we have been justified through faith, we have peace with God through our Lord Jesus Christ, through whom we have gained access by faith into this grace in which we now stand. And we rejoice in the hope of the glory of God." Paul got that answer from Someone—the same Someone who still hasn't retired from teaching His children!

Prayer

Amen. Praise to You, dear Lord. Amen.